Baby
Polar Bears

Mary Elizabeth Salzmann

Consulting Editor, Diane Craig, M.A./Reading Specialist

Sandcastle

An Imprint of Abdo Publishing
www.abdopublishing.com

www.abdopublishing.com

Published by Abdo Publishing, a division of ABDO, PO Box 398166, Minneapolis, Minnesota 55439. Copyright © 2015 by Abdo Consulting Group, Inc. International copyrights reserved in all countries. No part of this book may be reproduced in any form without written permission from the publisher. SandCastle™ is a trademark and logo of Abdo Publishing.

Printed in the United States of America, North Mankato, Minnesota

102014
012015

THIS BOOK CONTAINS
RECYCLED MATERIALS

Editor: Alex Kuskowski
Content Developer: Nancy Tuminelly
Cover and Interior Design and Production: Mighty Media, Inc.
Photo Credits: Shutterstock, Thinkstock

Library of Congress Cataloging-in-Publication Data

Salzmann, Mary Elizabeth, 1968- author.
  Baby polar bears / Mary Elizabeth Salzmann.
      pages cm. -- (Baby animals)
  Audience: Ages 4-9.
  ISBN 978-1-62403-511-1
1. Polar bear--Infancy--Juvenile literature. I. Title.
  QL737.C27S235 2015
  599.7861392--dc23
                                  2014023427

SandCastle™ Level: Beginning

SandCastle™ books are created by a team of professional educators, reading specialists, and content developers around five essential components—phonemic awareness, phonics, vocabulary, text comprehension, and fluency—to assist young readers as they develop reading skills and strategies and increase their general knowledge. All books are written, reviewed, and leveled for guided reading, early reading intervention, and Accelerated Reader® programs for use in shared, guided, and independent reading and writing activities to support a balanced approach to literacy instruction. The SandCastle™ series has four levels that correspond to early literacy development. The levels are provided to help teachers and parents select appropriate books for young readers.

EMERGING · **BEGINNING** · TRANSITIONAL · FLUENT

Contents

Baby Polar Bears

Baby polar bears are born in dens.

Most baby polar bears are **twins**.

Baby polar bears are white.

Baby polar bears follow their mother. She leads them to water.

Baby polar bears are good swimmers.

Baby polar bears learn to hunt seals. They sit by a hole in the ice. They wait for a seal to come out.

Baby polar bears have wide paws. This helps them walk on snow and ice.

Baby polar bears play with each other.

Baby polar bears stay with their mothers for two to three years.

Did You Know?

► Newborn polar bears weigh less than 2 pounds (900 g).

► Polar bears wash themselves after they eat.

► Polar bears' closest **relatives** are brown bears.

► Polar bears live for 25 to 30 years.

Polar Bear Quiz

Read each sentence below. Then decide whether it is true or false.

1. Baby polar bears are gray.

2. Baby polar bears follow their mother to water.

3. Baby polar bears are not good swimmers.

4. Baby polar bears learn to hunt seals.

5. Baby polar bears have wide paws.

Answers: 1. False 2. True 3. False 4. True 5. True

Glossary

relative – a person or animal connected with another by blood.

twins – two babies born to the same mother at the same birth.